ORGAN

Praise & Worship

Preludes, Offertories, and Postludes

Creative Organ Settings by FRED BOCK

Fred Bock Music Company

FOREWORD

I've not been this excited about a new organ book since the last time I did a new organ book! But this one is special, as the Church Lady says on *Saturday Night Live!* There must be 23,749 books of hymn arrangements for organ out there in musicland, but to my knowledge, there is no book like this one. The difference lies in the *treatments* that have been given to these Praise & Worship songs. The whole idea of Praise & Worship songs is a fairly new one, but in 1993, we find that more and more churches of all denominations are using these songs on a rather regular basis. These songs are no longer relegated to Youth services, singing around the campfire, or that 8 a.m. Sunday morning "contemporary" service. Out of about ten thousand Praise & Worship songs written over the last few years, the cream of the crop has risen to the top of the list. You can now hear Lutherans, Methodists and Presbyterians singing these songs as well as Baptists, Assemblies of God, and Nazarenes. The seven melodies I have chosen to create organ pieces on are popular just about everywhere. And even if your church has not yet gotten with it, (they will) when they do, some of these will be the very first ones they'll sing. For you to be able to play preludes, offertories, and postludes based on these popular hymns will make you a stellar, adroit, "with it" and way-ahead-of-your-time organist for sure.

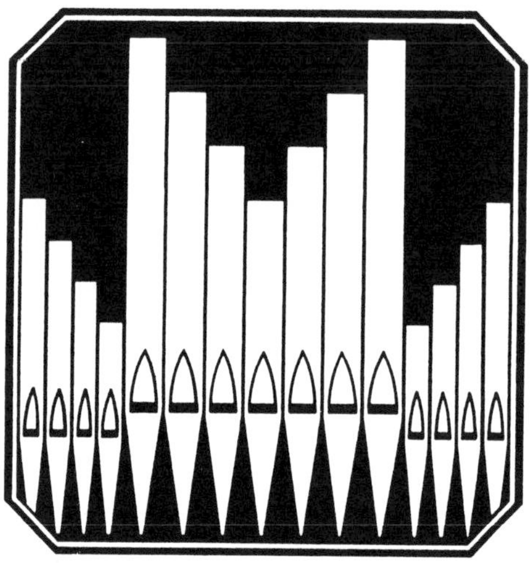

These seven pieces have been created to be through-composed pieces, not just hymn arrangements. The typical play a verse, play a verse in minor, modulate up a half-step hymn arrangement is not what these are all about. I set out to create a mood with each piece. You'll notice the upper left hand corner of each piece tells you how I see this piece best being used. (On the other hand, it's your book now, use the pieces as you wish!) The more festive settings (*We Will Glorify* and *He Is Exalted*) seem perfect for postludes on special days. The rest can readily be used for preludes or offertories, for weddings, funerals, etc., as you see fit. For concert use, or church bulletins, an alternate title is included for each title. (Thank you, Fred Tulan, for that good idea!)

My settings are easily detectable by their harmonic content. I've always enjoyed full, rich harmonies, and I guess it shows in my writing style. I've tried to create a welcome mix of styles and colors in these settings. For example, the mysterioso quality of *In My Life, Lord, Be Glorified,* is something I'm quite proud to have conceived. And the Vaughn-Williams/English-air quality of *I Love You, Lord,* also seems to me to make good sense as a treatment for this song. I just wanted them to be special, and definitely *not* typical hymn settings. Have I succeeded?

Might I offer a few suggestions as to how best to use these pieces in a service: get together with the minister or worship leader. Determine a theme or content topic for the service. Build from there. Say, for example, the theme is Worship and Adoration of God, a rather general, and useful theme. The congregation might sing *All Hail the Power of Jesus' Name,* and then perhaps a Praise & Worship song like *Majesty!* Follow that with a verse or two of *Praise to the Lord, the Almighty,* and finish up with *He is Exalted.* Now precede all that singing with organ preludes based on those songs and hymns, perhaps in the same sequence, ending with my setting of *He Is Exalted.* Prior to the morning prayer, have the choir sing *I Love You, Lord* (by the way, I also have a small collection of Praise & Worship songs arranged for use as choral responses, published by Fred Bock Music Company, octavo BG2213, entitled *Praise & Worship Choral Responses*). *I Love You, Lord,* as an organ offertory might then be a nice way to tie everything together in this service of praise. And, if your congregation sings *We Will Glorify,* then you'll have plenty of reason to finish up the service with a rousing organ postlude on the same title. See how this all ties together? I guarantee it will work at your church, too. Anything we do requires forethought and planning, and when the minister, minister of music, and organist all get their collective heads together for the purpose of uniting their congregation in worship, nothing but good can come from such a meeting.

Using Praise & Worship songs does not mean throwing away the hymnal in favor of overhead transparencies. Not at all! Integrating both old and new, when done in a spirit of unifying the worship service, brings people together. I wish you well, since for many this is venturing into new territory. And since we're only human, and we all like what we know best, those first steps can be mighty scary! My guess is that in years to come, some of these songs will be as beloved and popular as *Holy, Holy, Holy,* or even a newer hymn like *Lift High the Cross* are today: crossing all denominational and stylistic boundaries. I hope my book of organ settings will help you over the bridge.

Sincerely,

Fred

Fred Bock
Los Angeles, California
May, 1993

Postlude

For Fred Swann

WE WILL GLORIFY

(TOCCATA BRILLIANTE)

Sw. Full organ FF, 4′ coupler
and Mixtures (no reeds)
Gt. Full organ FFF, mixtures,
reeds, 4′ coupler
Ped. Full pedal 16′, 8′, 4′
Sw. to Ped. 8′

Twila Paris
Arranged by Fred Bock

Gt.
ff
Sw.
Gt.
legato
Sw.

Broaden
Gt.
solidly
a tempo

allargando
a tempo
sforzando on
ffff
white pedal
glissando

Prelude
Offertory
Communion

For Tom Hazelton

HE IS LORD

(MEDITATION ON AN AMERICAN MELODY)

Sw. Flute 4′
Ch. Strings 8′
String celestes 8′, 4′
Ped. Light Flute or String 16′, 8′

Traditional Melody
Arranged by Fred Bock

a little more movement
Add Ch. to Ch. 4′
Ch.
mf
off
Ch. to Ch. 4′

Sw.
Ch.
ad lib.
pp

Prelude
Offertory
Communion

For Chris Elliott

FATHER, I ADORE YOU

(CHORALE PRELUDE ON "ADORATION")

Sw. Gamba Celeste 8′ or French Horn 8′
or suitable solo stop
Prepare: Flute 4′
Ch. Strings 8′, 4′
Ped. Bourdon 16′, Gedeckt 8′
Ch. to Ped.

Terry Coehlo
Arranged by Fred Bock

Moderato-with expression

Ch.
Sw. Flute 4′
mf
a little brighter
Add Ch. to Ch. 4′
Ch.
mf

off Ch. to Ch. 4′
mp
Reduce pedal
pp

Prelude
Offertory

For Barbara Petker

HOLY, HOLY

(ADORATION ANTIPHON)

Sw. Nachthorn 4′
Prepare: Flutes 8′, 2′
Ch. Strings, Celestes 8′, 4′
Ped. Lieblich Gedeckt, Soft Flute 8′
Ch. to Ped. 8′

Jimmy Owens
Arranged by Fred Bock

Moderato, with freedom and expression

ten.
Ch.
mf
Flute chorus
Sw.
mf
ad lib.

l.h.
r.h.
Ch.
mp
Sw.
mf
Sw. (4′ solo)

Ch.
Ch. mf
ten.
mp
p
Reduce pedal

Prelude
Postlude

For Dan Miller

HE IS EXALTED

(TOCCATA JUBILATE)

Sw. Full, no reeds or mixtures
Gt. Full, with reeds and mixtures, no 16′
Ped. Diapasons, Flutes, 16′, 8′
Sw. to Ped. 8′
(to balance both manuals)
Add Gt. to Ped. later

Twila Paris
Arranged by Fred Bock

Allegro-with exuberance

simile
Sw.

Gt. or Reed 8′ (reed *not* coupled to Ped.)
Add Gt. to Ped. 8′(4′?)
Sw.

Gt.
Add Gt. to Gt. 4′
simile
Sw.
Gt.
sfz on
a tempo
no rit.
fff
Add 32′ pedal reed
ff

Prelude
Communion

For Kimo Smith

IN MY LIFE, LORD, BE GLORIFIED

(A SYLVAN POEME)

Sw. Clarinet 8′ or
Flute 4′
No tremolo
Gt. Sw. to Gt. 8′ (no stops)
Ch. Strings, Celestes 8′, (4′?)
Ped. Bourdon 16′, Lieblich Gedeckt 16′
Ch. to Ped. 8′

Bob Kilpatrick
Arranged by Fred Bock

a tempo
Ch.
a little brighter
Gt.
mf

Ch.
mp
mf
mf
mf
f

* Or play E with right thumb on Gt., and Ch. part on Sw.

Prelude
Offertory

For Jan Sanborn

I LOVE YOU, LORD

(BALLADE in F)

Sw. Oboe 8′, Light Reed 8′
or Flute 8 with Nazard 2 2/3′
Prepare: Flute 4′
Prepare: Flute 4′ - No tremolo
Ch. Flutes and Strings 8′, 4′
Ped. Lieblich Gedeckt 16′, Light Flute 8′

Laurie Klein
Arranged by Fred Bock

not rushed
Sw. Flute 4′
mf
3

ten.
mf
Ch.
ten.
not rushed
mf

Sw. Light Reed solo
mf
mp
legato

not rushed
Ch.
3
mf
mp
pp

Do You Have These Other Fred Bock Organ Books?

The Organ Music of Fred Bock #1

BG0889

Contents

Prelude on *BE THOU MY VISION*
Prelude on *JESUS, THOU JOY OF LOVING HEARTS*
Prelude on *THE LORD'S MY SHEPHERD*
Prelude on *MORNING HAS BROKEN*
Postlude on *NOW THANK WE ALL OUR GOD*
Fantasia on *ON CHRISTMAS NIGHT*

The Organ Music of Fred Bock #2

BG0914

Contents

ANGELS, FROM THE REALMS OF GLORY
ANGELS WE HAVE HEARD ON HIGH
I WONDER AS I WANDER
INFANT HOLY, INFANT LOWLY
JOY TO THE WORLD
O COME, ALL YE FAITHFUL
O LITTLE TOWN OF BETHLEHEM
SILENT NIGHT
THE FIRST NOEL
THOU DIDST LEAVE THY THRONE